ABC

Blessing

Book for

Girls

Books by Kathleen Miller

God's Heart: My Home

Dog Devotions

Hymns for the Heart Away from Home

Journaling the Journey
Accompanies Hymns for the Heart

The Cyrus Anointing for Today

Reflection Journal for
The Cyrus Anointing for Today

ABC Blessing Book for Boys

ABC Blessing Book for Girls

Books by Kathleen and Donald Miller

Explaining Salvation

Bible Memory Verse Games for Children

Little Books | Big Ideas

ABC
Blessing
Book for

Girls

Kathleen Miller

Cyrus CyberPublishing®

www.CyrusCyberPublishing.com

ABC BLESSING BOOK FOR GIRLS
by Kathleen Miller

www.ABCBLESSINGBOOKS.COM
© 2010 Kathleen Miller

Published by Cyrus CyberPublishing®
46 E Agate Avenue 913
Granby, CO 80446

Library of Congress Control Number: 2010918942
ISBN 978-0-9829435-9-5 Hardcover
1. Christian Living / Spiritual Growth / General

Printed in China through Four Colour Print Group
Louisville, Ketucky
CPSIA
Production Date   01/27/11
Plant & Location   Printed by Everbest Printing
                     Company, Nansha, China
Job/Batch #   99237

Design & Illustrations | Danielle Zacharias

Dedicated to

Blanch Hershberger

May you never cease to bless others.

Tiffany Hartzler

May you experience all these blessings.

So they shall put My name on the children...
and I will bless them.

Numbers 6:27

Contents

Preface

*E*ven before my children were born, I wanted them to experience the blessings of God. Being a teacher of literacy, I have frequently used the ABCs to teach basic concepts. I decided to write an ABC book to pass on the concept of blessing children.

As I wrote the lines for each letter, I asked three questions: What gifts or abilities did God give this woman? How did God help her? How did this woman help others? Answers to these questions are reflected in the blessings in this book.

Blessing children is something God wants us to do. Jesus demonstrated passing on the enabling of God on the lives of children. We should not be selfish with our time or our words and neglect to pass on the blessings of God. We need to remember that God is not a respecter of persons.

The blessings He gave women in the Bible represent gifts He wants to give today.

I want these blessings to be passed on to children. I wrote the *ABC Blessing Book for Girls* to help you do that. May the following be your prayer.

Prayer

Dear God,

I know children are important to You. Jesus told children to come to Him. He blessed them and said that the Kingdom of Heaven was theirs.[1]

Scripture says that we make choices by the words we speak.[2] I choose to speak words of blessings over *Child's Name*.

I speak these blessings believing *Child's Name* will experience the same abilities You gave other women in the Bible.[3] *Child's Name* will be blessed and so will I.[4]

Selah.

And He took them up in His arms,
laid His hands on them,
and blessed them.

Mark 10:16

Introduction

*G*od said that He would bless our children.[5] The purpose of the *ABC Blessing Book for Girls* is to pass on the blessings of God by applying the principles of tradition, choice, and faith.

Traditions have historically been passed on orally. When God gave Moses the *Book of the Law*, He did it by the spoken word.[6] Jewish culture gives precedence to oral traditions.[7] Speaking a blessing on children extends the belief that spoken words are powerful.[8] When God created the world He spoke it into existence.[9] The powers of life and death are passed on through words. The words we speak shape lives and destinies.[10]

God told us to choose this day whom we would serve.[11] The choice is a decision we make daily. Speaking blessings upon our children guides them in choices they make and paths they follow. What we say over their lives does affect them.[12]

Finally, pronouncing blessings affirms our faith.[13] We pass on our trust in God to children when we speak biblical blessings on their lives.[14] We believe that what God did for others, He will do for them.[15] Our children learn to sense God's power and enabling in their lives, as well as our confidence in Him.[16] They come to know the God who blessed Sarah, Esther, and Lydia as the God who blesses them.

The descriptions of the women in this book do not portray a complete picture of their character or deeds. They are included to provide scriptural support for the blessing that God gave each one.

Enjoy reading the *ABC Blessing Book for Girls*. Be assured that as you bless children you a pleasing God.[17]

A

May God bless you as Abigail.
You understand others and see
what to do.

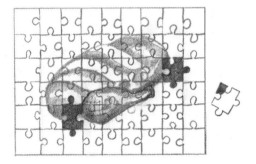

A is for Abigail.

Abigail was a woman of good understanding and beauty. Her wisdom was greater than the foolishness of her husband. She was rewarded by the hand of David.

B

Bathsheba

May God bless you as Bathsheba.
You are beautiful and charming.

B is for Bathsheba.

Bathsheba was a beautiful woman who captivated King David's attention. She became his wife and the mother of Solomon. She experienced God's forgiveness and blessings.

C

Chloe

May God bless you as Chloe.
You are a friend to many.

C is for Chloe.

Chloe was one of the early Christians of the church. She was known for hospitality, peace, and good judgment.

D

Deborah

May God bless you as Deborah.
You know the difference between
right and wrong.

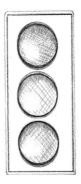

D is for Deborah.

Deborah was a wise judge and a courageous woman.

E

Elisabeth

May God bless you as Elisabeth.
You comfort others with your
kindness.

E is for Elisabeth.

Elisabeth spiritually wrapped Mary in a blanket of comfort. She was the mother of John the Baptist and the cousin of Mary, who became the mother of Jesus.

F

Friend

May God bless you as His friend. You talk to Him and hear Him talk to you.

F is for friend.

God sent His Son to lay down his life for his friends. We are his friends.

G

Grace

May God bless you with grace.
You feel God accepting you with
His love.

G is for grace.

Grace is the goodness that God gives us. It is the goodness we do not deserve.

H

Hannah

May God bless you as Hannah.
You share the gifts God gives you.

H is for Hannah.

Hannah gave back to God the gift of a son. His name was Samuel.

I

Iscah

May God bless you as Iscah.
You delight in the home God gives
you.

I is for Iscah.

Iscah was the niece of Abraham. Iscah had the opportunity to look forward to a city whose builder was God.

J

Jochebed

May God bless you as Jochebed.
You trust God to protect those you
love.

J is for Jochebed.

Jochebed was the mother of Moses. She hid him in the Nile River. Pharaoh's daughter found him and saved him from being killed.

K

Kezia

May God bless you as Kezia.
Your beauty is noticed among
those around you.

K is for Kezia.

Kezia was a daughter of Job after all had been taken from him. It was said that no women were as fair as the daughters of Job.

L

Lydia

May God bless you as Lydia.

You make wise decisions that bring good things.

L is for Lydia.

Lydia was prosperous. She was a diligent woman in business.

M

Mary

May God bless you as Mary.
You are willing to do what God
plans for you.

M is for Mary.

Mary responded to God, *Let it be to me according to Your word.* She was the mother of Jesus.

N

Naomi

May God bless you as Naomi.
You accept the help you need from others.

N is for Naomi.

Naomi accepted the help and kindness of Ruth who was her daughter-in-law.

O

Only One

May God bless you as His only one.

You are unique and special to Him.

O is for the only one.

Only one person is like you. God made no one to take your place.

P

Phoebe

May God bless you as Phoebe.
You help others and they help you.

P is for Phoebe.

Phoebe served in the church with vigor. The Apostle Paul asked others to assist her with anything she needed because she was so helpful.

Q

Queen Esther

May God bless you as Queen Esther.

You have the courage to do the right thing.

Q is for Queen Esther.

Queen Esther risked her life to go before the king and ask him to protect her people.

R

Ruth

May God bless you as Ruth.
You are loyal and God rewards
your helping hands and kind heart.

R is for Ruth.

Ruth was loyal to her mother-in-law. God blessed Ruth by having Boaz marry and take care of her, thereby placing her in the lineage of Jesus.

S

Sarah

May God bless you as Sarah.
You enjoy what God promises you.

S is for Sarah.

Sarah was promised a son, and even though she laughed when she heard, she later enjoyed her son named Isaac.

T

Tryphena

May God bless you as Tryphena.
You are a diligent worker.

T is for Tryphena.

Tryphena worked hard for the Lord.

U

Unselfish

May God bless you as unselfish.
You love others as you love
yourself.

U is for Unselfish.

You are not selfish. You love others and you love yourself.

V

Vashti

May God bless you as Vashti.
You shine your light of virtue.

V is for Vashti.

Vashti refused to be treated as an immoral person. She maintained respect and dignity for herself as a woman.

W

Woman

May God bless you as a woman.
You trust Him as your Maker.

W is for woman.

A woman is the creation of God. He made her special.

X

eXceedingly

May God bless you eXceedingly.
You are happy and full of joy.

X is for eXceedingly.

The eXceeding joy of God in your life overflows on others and makes them happy.

Y

You

May God bless you as you.
You are free to be yourself.

Y is for you.

You have the faith to be you. God helps you be the person He created you to be.

Z

Zibiah

May God bless you as Zibiah.
You cheer others to do good
things.

Z is for Zibiah.

Zibiah was the mother of a noble son. He heeded instruction to do what was right in the sight of the Lord.

Epilogue

The Lord bless you and keep you; the Lord make his face shine upon you and be gracious to you; the Lord lift His countenance upon you, and give you peace. This scripture recorded in Numbers 6:24-26 has become a mantra. God told Moses to bless the people in this way. May we do the same.

Notes

1. Mark 10:13-16

2. Proverbs 18:21

3. John 16:23-24

4. Genesis: 22: 17

5. Ephesians 1:3; Deuteronomy 28:1-14

6. Exodus 34:27

7. Elman, Y & Gershoni, I Eds. (2000). *Transmitting Jewish traditions: reality, textuality and cultural diffusion*. New Haven, CT: Yale Press.

8. Hebrews 11:13

9. John 1:1-3; Genesis 1; Psalm 33:9

10. Proverbs 18:21

11. Deuteronomy 30:19-20

12. Proverbs 12:14

13. II Corinthians 4:13

14. Deuteronomy 11:19, 21

15. Romans 2:11

16. Isaiah 44:3

17. Deuteronomy 28:1-2

References for Blessings

Abigail: I Samuel 25:1-42

Bathsheba: II Samuel 12:24

Chloe: I Corinthians 1:11

Deborah: Judges 4-5

Elisabeth: Luke 1:5-80

Friend: John 15:13; Psalm 18:24

Grace: II Peter 3:18

Hannah: I Samuel 1:11-28

Iscah: Genesis 11:29; Hebrews 11:30

Jochebed: Exodus 2:1-11

Kezia: Job 42:15

Lydia: Acts 16:14-15

Mary: Luke 1:38

Naomi: Ruth 1-2

One: Psalm 139:13-16

Phoebe: Roman 16:1-2

Queen Esther: Esther 2-9

Ruth: Ruth 1-4; Matthew 1:5

Sarah: Genesis 18:12-14

Tryphena: Romans 16:12

Unselfish: Matthew 22:39

Vashti: Esther 1:10-12

Woman: Genesis 3:20-22

eXceedingly: Ephesians 3:20

You: John 8:32,36

Zibiah: II Chronicles 24:1-2

The Author

$\mathcal{K}$athleen Miller has wanted to bless children since she was a little girl. When she was five she would line up chairs and put her dolls and stuffed animals on them. She used a blackboard mounted on the concrete wall to teach them what she knew. Back then she did not know much about the lives of women mentioned in *ABC Blessing Book for Girls*, but she wanted to share what she knew.

Today she knows more and has experienced teaching populations that extend beyond those that sat on the little chairs in the basement. Kathleen has taught students in the United States and Mexico, in special reading classes, English as a Second Language (ESL) classes, elementary school, middle school, and high school. At the university and college levels, she has taught literacy courses to undergraduate and graduate students.

Kathleen has written numerous books and articles. She has been published in campus and community newspapers, a music magazine, and an educational journal. She writes curricula for developing reading, writing, and English language skills.

On an academic note, Kathleen has a PhD and an MA in Reading Education, an MA in Teaching English as a Second Language, and a BA in Elementary Education.

Kathleen Miller is a wife, mother, educator, and writer. She has been the helpmate of a missionary, associate pastor, and children's pastor. Her sons are now both grown, but she continues to pray the blessings of God on their lives. Through her words and actions Kathleen believes God blesses lives today.

Acknowledgments

Grateful I am.

God has blessed me with family and friends who have supported my efforts in writing this book.

Donald Miller provided scriptures that are the basis for this book.

Blanch Hershberger welcomed the purpose of these blessings and gave suggestions for the layout.

Becky Hartzler applauded the manuscript and offered ideas for the images.

LaWanda Miller assisted with content and copyediting.

Reita Yoder once again shared her wisdom and grace.

Carol Craig-Williams cheered me with courage and kindness.

Jay Hartzler believed in me and sponsored this project.

I thank God for these people who helped me with this book.

Share your stories of being blessed
and blessing others.

Blessings@ABCBlessingBooks.com